6/03

TCHAIKOVSKY

For my Nannie - Edna May Kenney
whose life has been devoted to other people's babies.

First edition for the United States, Canada,
and the Philippines published 1993
by Barron's Educational Series, Inc.

Design David West Children's Book Design

Designed and produced by
Aladdin Books Ltd
28 Percy Street
London W1P 9FF

All inquiries should be addressed to:
Barron's Educational Series, Inc.
250 Wireless Boulevard
Hauppauge, NY 11788

International Standard Book No. 0-8120-1545-2

Library of Congress Catalog Card No. 92-29832

Library of Congress Cataloging-in-Publication Data
Rachlin, Ann.
     Tchaikovsky / by Ann Rachlin ; illustrated by Susan Hellard. –1st
ed. for the U.S., Canada, and the Philippines.
       p. cm. – (Famous children)
   Summary: A biography of the nineteenth-century Russian composer
with emphasis on his childhood and early musical training.
   ISBN 0-8120-1545-2
   1. Tchaikovsky, Peter Ilich, 1840-1893–Childhood and youth–
Juvenile literature. 2. Composers–Russia–Biography–Juvenile
literature.[1. Tchaikovsky, Peter Ilich, 1840-1893–Childhood and
youth. 2. Composers.] I. Hellard, Susan. ill. II. Series:
Rachlin, Ann. Famous people.
ML3930.C4R3 1993
780'.92–dc20
[B]   92-29832
                                          CIP
                                        AC MN

Printed in Belgium   14 13 12 11 10 9 8 7 6 5

Famous Children

TCHAIKOVSKY

Ann Rachlin
illustrated by Susan Hellard

BARRON'S

"Goodbye, Mama! Goodbye, Nikolai! Come back soon!" The two children waved as the carriage disappeared around the corner. Little Peter had tears in his eyes.

"When will she be back?" he asked his father.

"She won't be long," said Mr. Tchaikovsky. "Mama's taking Nikolai to St. Petersburg to find you a governess. Don't look so sad, Peter!"

Peter's little sister Sasha seemed to have already forgotten Mama. Suddenly Peter stood still.

"Sasha," he called. "I've got a great idea. Let's make up a song for Mama. We can sing it to her when she comes back. We'll call it *Our Mama in St. Petersburg*!" And he started to hum the tune.

"They're here!" The sound of the carriage wheels brought everyone out of the house. Peter ran to Mama and she picked him up and hugged him. The courtyard was crowded with happy people as everyone rushed to welcome Mama home.

"This is Fanny, our new governess," said Mama to Papa. Mr. Tchaikovsky greeted Fanny warmly.

"I hope you will be very happy with us, Fanny," he said.

The next morning Fanny began to teach the older children, Nikolai and his cousin Lydia. Fanny was a good teacher and lessons were fun.

"Why can't I have lessons, Fanny?" pleaded Peter.

"Because you are too little!" Every day Peter came to Fanny's schoolroom until one morning she said, with a sigh, "Oh very well, Peter. You can have lessons too."

Peter adored Fanny and enjoyed his lessons. Soon he could read and write better than his elder brother. But he was so messy! He never tied his shoelaces. His shirt was always buttoned the wrong way. There was dirt on his trousers and his hands were always grubby.

"Just look at you, Peter," said Fanny, as she smoothed his uncombed hair. "You're a mess!"

One morning, Peter was alone in the nursery. Suddenly he heard the sound of galloping horses and he rushed to the window. The winter snow lay thick on the ground. A-gallop, a-gallop, a-gallop, a-gallop!

The rhythm of the horses' hooves sounded like music to Peter and he tapped in time on the window. The louder the sounds, the harder he hit the glass. Suddenly it shattered as his little hand went through the windowpane. He screamed.

F anny and Mama washed and bandaged his hand.

"Why did you break the window, Peter?" asked Mama.

"It was the music of the horses," explained Peter.

"What horses?" asked Fanny. She carried Peter to the window. There were no hoofprints in the smooth white snow.

"You had better have piano lessons," said Mama. "The next time you hear 'the music of the horses' you can play it instead on the piano. It will be less dangerous."

The house was quiet. The grown-ups had been dancing to the music of Papa's player piano. When Papa changed the music rolls, Peter would run to his piano and pick out the tunes. Later that evening, as Fanny came upstairs, she heard Peter crying.

"This music! It won't let me sleep!" Fanny tried to calm him.

"There is no music, Peter. Everyone's gone home."

"It's here," said Peter, pointing to his head. "I can't get rid of it. It won't leave me alone."

Papa had a new job and the whole family was moving to Moscow. Fanny was not going with them. There were tears in her eyes as she kissed the sleeping children goodbye. When Peter realized she had gone, he was very sad. He tried to write her a letter, but he cried so much that the pen made five blots on the paper and he had to start again.

When they arrived in Moscow, someone else had taken Papa's new job.

"Let's go to St. Petersburg!" said Mama. "Nikolai and Peter can go to the Schmelling School there."

The family did as Mama suggested, but Peter hated school. And there was too much homework. Sometimes he did not finish until midnight. So he was quite happy when one morning he woke up covered with red spots. He had caught the measles.

The measles made Peter very ill and he had to stay at home. His mother found a new governess for him, named Anastasia. Peter's mother wrote to Fanny,

"Dear and good Fanny, Although I am satisfied with Anastasia, the children are not the same as when they were with you, especially Peter. He has become impatient and he answers back and cries whenever he is told to do something he does not like. I hope he will grow out of it before he goes to boarding school."

Boarding school! Whenever he thought of it, Peter trembled with fear and hurried to the piano. He was a very frail and sensitive child – "made of china," Fanny had said.

"I am always at the piano," he wrote to her. "It cheers me up when I am sad."

In September 1850, when he was ten years old, Peter started in the preparatory class of the School of Law in St. Petersburg. Peter was very lonely without Nikolai, who had been sent to a different school. The family now lived far away but Mama stayed in St.Petersburg while he was getting settled.

Peter clung to his mother's hand. A few tears ran down his cheeks but he was calm. They were traveling to the Central Turnpike where Mama would board the coach to return home. Their friend Mr. Keiser had brought his two children to keep Peter company. When Mama left, he would take Peter and the children back to school.

"Be a brave boy, Peter." Mama kissed him goodbye. Peter burst into tears and clung to her.

"No, no, darling, don't cry. I'll be back soon." But Peter sobbed as though his heart would break. Mr. Keiser had to drag him away from his mother, who climbed into the coach.

The horses started to move. With a cry of despair, Peter pulled away from Mr. Keiser and rushed after the carriage. He grabbed at the footboard and slipped as his hand touched the wheels.

"Don't go! Don't go!" he screamed. Strong arms lifted him up. Mr. Keiser tried to comfort him. Bruised and covered with mud, Peter Tchaikovsky sobbed as he watched the coach disappear down the road.

The teachers at his new school were kind to Peter. Monsieur Berrard, his French teacher, even took him to the Children's Court Ball where he saw the Tsar – the ruler of the mighty Russian empire.

"He was as close as the sofa is to the writing desk in Papa's study," he wrote to his parents. Peter missed them. They kept promising to come and see him, but something always prevented them.

"If my beautiful angels do not come," he wrote, "I will be very lonely."

It was Sunday and Peter lifted his books out of the hollow linden tree in the garden. Instead of going out to see Nikolai, he had to stay at school and study.

"I was third in the February exams," he thought. "I'm sure I'll do well in the ones in June too."

Peter was right. He passed the exams and went into the advanced School of Law. His parents had decided he would be a lawyer. The boys liked him, especially when he played the piano for them to dance. One day the noise of their stamping feet disturbed Monsieur Berrard in the room below. When he angrily opened the door, the boys rushed out. Peter refused to give their names and took the punishment alone. Monsieur Berrard shook his head sadly. "Peter, you are one of our best students, but I fear that music will always be your first love."

Monsieur Berrard was right. Some years later, Peter decided to become a musician. He went on to write ten operas, six symphonies, four concertos, and the music for three famous ballets:

The Sleeping Beauty

Swan Lake

The Nutcracker